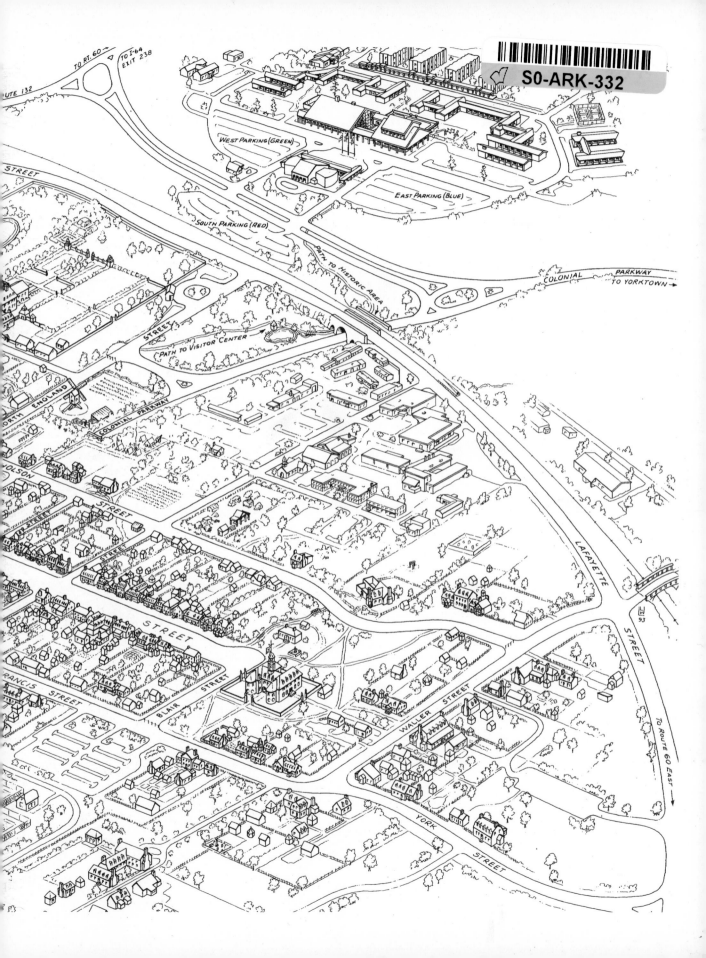

S0-ARK-332

The Majesty of Colonial Williamsburg

The Majesty of
COLONIAL
WILLIAMSBURG

Photography and text by Peter Beney

in association with
The Colonial Williamsburg Foundation

PELICAN PUBLISHING COMPANY
Gretna 1997

Copyright © 1997
By Peter Beney
All rights reserved

*The word "Pelican" and the depiction of a pelican are trademarks
of Pelican Publishing Company, Inc.
and are registered in the U.S. Patent and Trademark Office.*

Library of Congress Cataloging-in-Publication Data

Beney, Peter.
    The majesty of Colonial Williamsburg / photography and text by Peter
Beney.
        p.   cm.
    ISBN 0-88289-993-7 (hc : alk. paper). — ISBN 1-56554-249-5 (pb : alk.
paper)
    1. Williamsburg (Va.)—Pictorial works. 2. Historic buildings—Virginia—
Williamsburg—Pictorial works. I. Title.
F234.W7.B445 1997
975.5'4252—dc20   96-41796
                                                                              CIP

Photo on p. 2: Carter's Grove mansion
Photo on p. 6: Sign outside Shields Tavern
Photo on p. 8: Shields Tavern
Photo on p. 10: Bassett Hall
Photo on p. 176: Flowers
Map by Louis Luedtke

Book design by Dana Bilbray

Printed in Hong Kong

Published by Pelican Publishing Company, Inc.
1101 Monroe Street, Gretna, Louisiana 70053

To Frank McGuire
For his inspiration, interest, and support in my publishing career

Acknowledgments

My thanks to the Colonial Williamsburg Foundation for making this publication possible. My thanks also to Joseph N. Rountree, Director of Publications; Susan M. Stuntz, Vice-President of Marketing Communications; John O. Sands, Director of Administration, Collections and Museums Division; Betty Leviner, Curator of Exhibition Buildings; Orene Coffman at the Williamsburg Inn; and all the curators, interpreters, and staff in the Historic Area who escorted me and provided information. My thanks to Louise Kelley, Manager, Carter's Grove and Bassett Hall, and for the help of Louise Lambert Kale, Executive Director of the Historic Campus at the College of William and Mary, and for the generosity of all the other people who gave their time and very useful information for the production of this book.

My special thanks to Patrick R. Saylor, Public Relations Manager at Colonial Williamsburg, who worked very closely with me on this project. He made all the arrangements for me to photograph the buildings and tradespeople, provided me with unlimited detailed information, and arrived at the crack of dawn with keys to open buildings for early morning photo sessions on numerous occasions.

My thanks also to the staff at Pelican Publishing Company and in particular to Ashley Ellington for her editorial input and Dana Bilbray for the design of this book.

Contents

Preface

The significance of Williamsburg to the history of the United States was recognized by John D. Rockefeller, Jr., in 1926. First suggested to him by the Reverend Dr. W. A. R. Goodwin, the opportunity to preserve 88 original buildings and re-create this remarkable community for everyone to enjoy became one of his priorities. Rockefeller lavished his vision, energy, and wealth on the reconstruction of buildings that were all but lost to decay and neglect. He personally oversaw the accurate rebirth of Williamsburg; using every modern technological means available at that time, he nurtured an army of archaeologists, architects, and artisans through their research and renovation of this historic treasure.

Today the Colonial Williamsburg Foundation maintains this eighteenth-century capital of colonial Virginia and continues to refine its authenticity almost daily. The result of this painstaking re-creation is enjoyed by millions of visitors who come to Williamsburg to see the buildings, eat at the taverns, and ride in carriages through its peaceful streets. An atmosphere of colonial lifestyle evokes a vivid and romantic period in our history which, while contrasting dramatically with today's standards, offers a measure of entertainment as it promotes appreciation for present-day principles.

The importance of Colonial Williamsburg as a place of education can be judged by the fact that many of our basic rights and codes have their foundation here. In Williamsburg, Virginia colonists developed principles of self-government, individual liberty, and responsible leadership.

One cannot help leaving this place feeling both enlightened and grateful. Without the events that took place here two and a half centuries ago, this great nation would not have taken the shape it has today. As inevitable as colonial independence must have been, it may not have affected history so kindly under the control of lesser men.

Introduction

Under the auspicious sponsorship of the Virginia Company of London, 104 men and boys sailed across the Atlantic Ocean in three ships, arriving after many hardships and storms on April 26, 1607. Seventeen days later, they established a settlement on the largest river in Chesapeake Bay. They named their settlement Jamestown and the river the James River after their king, James I. For the next three years these and subsequent settlers struggled to maintain the settlement. Although the Powhatan Indians sometimes supplied the newcomers with food and showed them how to grow corn and find fresh water, the settlers endured privations. During a period called the "Starving Time," 440 out of the 500 settlers died from disease, starvation, and the lack of clean fresh water.

By 1610, the remaining settlers were tired of struggling and were ready to leave. Just in time, a ship arrived from England with additional men and supplies. With new hope in their hearts the settlers remained. The marriage of one colonist, John Rolfe, to Powhatan's daughter Pocahontas brought several years of peace with the Indians, and Rolfe's cultivation of West Indian tobacco in Virginia soil brought economic success to the colony. Despite problems within the Virginia Company in England and a devastating Indian attack against the settlers in 1622, the colony survived. In 1624, King James dissolved the Virginia Company. The following year Virginia became a royal colony.

Middle Plantation had been established farther south, on the peninsula between the James and York rivers. This community included a small number of dwellings, a tavern, and Bruton Parish Church, which was the center of an early Anglican diocese. In 1693, by decree of King William III, the College of William and Mary was chartered. Established as what was described at the time "an intellectual haven in the wilderness of the New World," the new building, called simply "the College," was built in 1695 at Middle Plantation.

After the Statehouse in Jamestown had been deliberately burned down by rebel Nathaniel Bacon, the decision was made to move the capital to Middle Plantation in 1699. Renamed Williamsburg, this new location was considered a much healthier environment for a major center of commerce and government. Situated on higher ground, it had a cooler climate and fewer problems than the mosquito-infested low country marshes of Jamestown. "The College" was the most prominent building at the time and was deemed suitable for governmental meetings, so the General Assembly quickly established itself there—much to the disturbance of college business, it was recorded.

Williamsburg, so named in honor of King William III, was planned and laid out to reflect the beliefs of the time that cities should be centers of government, learning, and religion. The town was designed in a grid pattern with dimensions that were one mile by one-half mile. Open spaces, a green, and a square gave an air of uncrowded elegance. Small fenced meadows for farm animals and well-kept gardens gave it a pastoral aspect. With the College of William and Mary already established at one end of the town to the west and the parish church located midway, the new Capitol building was constructed on the eastern end to complete the formula. A thoroughfare connecting these important components was named "Duke of Gloucester Street." It is a very impressive main street by eighteenth-century colonial standards, being nearly one mile long and ninety-nine feet wide.

Over the next few years more public buildings were erected; as Williamsburg grew, it also became necessary to build more taverns and many more houses to accommodate the population. Construction of a new Capitol building was begun first, in 1701, followed immediately by a Public Gaol, and then a residence for the governor. The Courthouse (at its first location) came next. That very same year a Magazine was erected to protect the town's muskets and powder. Built of brick, these buildings were all completed by 1722, thus establishing the capital of the Virginia colony as a city positioned to govern itself and ward off its enemies. Menace of attack from both the Indians and the Spanish still lingered over the community.

It was not until much later, in 1773, that the Public Hospital was constructed along the same brick-built lines. Some private dwellings, such as the Lightfoot House and the George Wythe House, were also built in imposing Georgian brick style, but many of the taverns and houses were of simpler construction. Built of timber frame and siding with shingles on their roofs, many of these dwellings were subjected to additions and alterations over the years. Although the brick buildings were intended to be more permanent, some additions were deemed necessary. A strong wall was constructed around the Magazine, and the Governor's Palace was found to need repair. Restorations ensued, which seemed like a good excuse to lavish the Palace with additional refinements. A ballroom and supper room were added to keep up with British society.

Outside the city, wealthy plantation owners followed suit and constructed their homes in brick also. An excellent example of this is Carter's Grove, which was built by Carter Burwell between 1750 and 1755 to demonstrate the planter's prosperity. There are many other examples of magnificent original plantation houses all up and down the James River.

Dormer windows.

Ordinary colonial working people, on the other hand, lived in more primitive dwellings. However, as wealth grew, particularly amongst the tradesmen, homes did become more elaborate. Evidence of this can be observed in the fine furniture and paintings people acquired over the years. Outbuildings were constructed to accommodate all domestic services—such as cooking and laundry—and the slaves that provided them.

Many new residents were skilled tradespeople emigrating from Britain in search of fortune in the New World. The original concept of the Virginia Company had been to encourage settlement by people who were seeking their fortune, unlike in other colonies where people were mainly escaping persecution. As the population in the colony grew Virginia supported an increasing number of artisans and tradespeople.

England then imposed a "stamp tax," which was a duty levied on many goods purchased within the colony.The mother country was in debt from fighting the Seven Years' War (called the French and Indian War in the colonies) in Europe and North America, and British politicians believed it fair to ask the colonists to bear some of the costs for their defense. Steadfastly maintaining that only the colonists' elected representatives, not Parliament, had the legal right to tax the settlers, Patrick Henry introduced resolutions against the Stamp Act in the House of Burgesses. The burgesses adopted several of Henry's resolutions and the governor dissolved the house.

Ultimately, Parliament repealed the Stamp Act, but the relationship between Virginia and England had begun to crack. Four years later, when another governor dissolved the House of Burgesses for opposing the Townshend Duties, the burgesses simply moved down the street to the Raleigh Tavern and continued their business in the Apollo Room. With each successive crisis, the distance between England and Virginia widened. Over time, these stresses led to open revolt and the American Revolution.

Virginia broke its allegiance to the crown and many of Williamsburg's prominent figures became directly involved in both the signing of the Declaration of Independence and the American Revolution. Patrick Henry, an early protester, became first governor of the new Commonwealth of Virginia. George Wythe, mentor and law professor of Thomas Jefferson, signed the

13

historic document. Thomas Jefferson, also a Declaration signer, later became governor of Virginia also. George Washington, who defeated Cornwallis and his British army at Yorktown, returned with his victorious American militia men through Williamsburg after accepting Cornwallis's unconditional surrender on October 19, 1781.

By then Williamsburg's era as a capital city was over. In 1780, Governor Thomas Jefferson had relocated Virginia's capital to Richmond for strategic reasons. The community survived as a market town, however, and because it still had the College of William and Mary, also remained a great center for education. The Public Hospital also stayed open.

The Civil War brought troops from both sides to Williamsburg and Union soldiers burned the College building, which could not be rebuilt until after the war.

The Reverend Dr. W. A. R. Goodwin was rector of Bruton Parish Church from 1903 to 1907. During his time in Williamsburg, Dr. Goodwin had been impressed by the important role his community had played in the American Revolution and was intrigued by the many eighteenth-century buildings that still remained. When he returned to Williamsburg in 1923, Goodwin was alarmed to find the twentieth century encroaching on the "memorials" of the town's Revolutionary past. He persuaded the philanthropist John D. Rockefeller, Jr., to become involved in his vision to revive Williamsburg. In 1926, restoration and reconstruction of the major elements of this historic city began. Rockefeller funded the project and gave it his enthusiastic support for thirty years. He and his wife Abby set up residence here in Bassett Hall, where they would live for long periods of time in order to be on hand for consultations regarding the reconstruction.

Abby Aldrich Rockefeller moved much of her beloved folk art to their new Williamsburg home; this collection has remained in Williamsburg to become the nucleus for a folk art museum, which is named after her.

All of Williamsburg's important public buildings, as well as the College of William and Mary's Wren Building and President's House, were either restored or rebuilt. The aim was to return every structure in the city to its original eighteenth-century appearance. Using information obtained from old documents, records, plans, drawings, and inventories, it was possible, with

Roses.

Hollyhocks.

the assistance of a large number of archaeologists, architects, and skilled craftsmen, to accomplish this task.

Today the Historic Area is run by the Colonial Williamsburg Foundation, which is trustee of an endowment provided by John D. Rockefeller, Jr. The Foundation provides what seems like an inexhaustible supply of research and education, together with an aggressive program for restoration to ensure that Colonial Williamsburg continues to improve the accuracy of the picture of the colonial past presented to the visitor.

Despite the fact that millions of people visit Williamsburg every year, a peaceful, eighteenth-century atmosphere is maintained. Closed to motor traffic during daylight hours, only horse-drawn carriages and bicycles are permitted in the streets. This makes walking here a very pleasant experience. With virtually no hills and something to see on every corner, the town is indeed accessible and interesting to young and old alike. The gardens are spectacular in spring and summer and a market in the center of town is open weekends in spring and fall and every day during the summer. Visitors to the buildings are greeted by well-informed interpreters who, dressed in period costume, recall the history of the buildings and the colonial figures connected with them. Throughout the Historic Area, trade sites are open for lessons in eighteenth-century ingenuity and accomplishment. Working during daylight hours and using only the tools and materials of the period, a dedicated team of craftsmen and -women produces beautiful handmade items.

Completing this exciting picture of Colonial Williamsburg are the carriage and wagon rides and reenactments by the militia, which drills on Market Square. A Fife and Drum corps also marches down Duke of Gloucester Street in the afternoon sunshine several times a week during the summer. For the public's enjoyment, taverns serve "colonial" fare and stores sell colonial-style goods. Refreshments of lemonade in summer and hot cider in winter, together with cookies and cakes, are available at locations throughout the Historic Area including Market Square. Merchants Square, which is located to the west of the Historic Area near the College of William and Mary, provides an opportunity for visitors to browse elegant, well-stocked stores selling very high quality products. Here the visitor will find dining to suit all tastes ranging from hamburgers and sandwiches to the finest gourmet dishes in restaurants that provide indoor and outdoor seating. The Williamsburg Theatre, where art and classic movies are presented daily, is also here.

Colonial Williamsburg's Visitor Center, located one-half mile away from the Historic Area, also has a theater where a short orientation film about the beginnings, history, and re-creation of the town can be seen. Adjoining the theater are exhibition halls with a model of Williamsburg and photographs of the various attractions.

Tickets may be purchased to enter the many colonial buildings and trade sites, but there is no charge to walk through the streets of the Historic Area or to visit the many colonial stores and taverns.

Transportation between the Visitor Center and the Historic Area is provided to ticket holders in the form of a bus service. For those preferring to walk, there is a long path though woodlands. It is certainly not practical to take a motor vehicle into Colonial Williamsburg; because of this, a large parking lot has been provided at the Visitor Center. It makes sense therefore to abandon your car for the day and enjoy the freedom of walking in this beautiful re-creation of the eighteenth century.

Store window.

The Majesty of Colonial Williamsburg

The front of the Wren Building faces east. Although not located within the boundaries of Colonial Williamsburg itself, the Wren Building, at the College of William and Mary, was erected between 1695 and 1700 and is the oldest academic building in use in English America. Its design, which may have been influenced by Sir Christopher Wren was, to quote the vernacular of the period, "adapted to the Nature of the Country." This building has survived the ravages of two wars and three fires. It was restored through the benevolence of John D. Rockefeller, Jr., between the years 1928 and 1931 as part of the Colonial Williamsburg restoration.

Wren Building
College of William and Mary

The College of William and Mary in Virginia was chartered on February 8, 1693, by England's King William III and Queen Mary II. It was established on 330 acres of land purchased at Middle Plantation, which later became Williamsburg, as "an intellectual haven in the wilderness of the New World."

The college celebrates more than three centuries of select academic education and is associated with such famous historical figures as George Washington, Thomas Jefferson, Peyton Randolph, Carter Henry Harrison, John Tyler, Jr., and Edmund Randolph.

The foundation for the first building, which was known simply as "the College," was laid in 1695. The capital of Virginia was moved from Jamestown to the village of Middle Plantation, which was renamed Williamsburg, in 1699. Over the next four years, until lawmakers moved into the uncompleted Capitol building in 1704, the College, being the largest and most prominent structure in the new city, was used as the meeting place of Virginia's House of Burgesses. In the years that followed, fire ravaged the building on three different occasions and subsequent reconstructions changed the architectural appearance many times. In 1705 fire nearly destroyed the whole building; four years later the Council voted to rebuild the structure using the existing walls. Between 1747 and 1752 the building was again used for government meetings. After the Battle of Yorktown in 1781, the French Army used it as a hospital. It was also put to similar use by the Confederate Army during the Civil War.

As the campus grew, "the College" was renamed the "Old Main Building." On February 8, 1859, the 166th anniversary of the college's founding, another fire damaged the building. Spreading from the chemistry laboratory, it destroyed the chapel and library. In 1862, the restored building was alllegedly burned by Union soldiers and remained closed for the duration of the Civil War.

The years after the Civil War brought austerity to the college, but its president, Benjamin Stoddert Ewell, refused to permit his institution to perish. Although there were only a few students attending and no formal classes were being held, he still faithfully rang the college's bell to commence each fall semester, and thus kept the college spirit alive. Eventually state and federal funds were procured to reopen the college in 1888.

In the early twentieth century the "Old Main Building" became known as the Wren Building because of references to the "Building" by a mathematics professor at the college, the Reverend Hugh Jones, in his 1724 publication, *The Present State of Virginia*. There he wrote that the "Building's" architecture was not unlike Chelsea Hospital in England. Today, however, many scholars question the Wren attribution.

When it was decided to re-create colonial Williamsburg, philanthropist John D. Rockefeller, Jr., proposed to restore "the College" and retain all of its eighteenth-century features. Extensive archaeological research was carried out to ensure the accuracy of the building, which was restored in 1928-31. The Wren Building is open daily to the public; guided tours explaining its rich history are available.

In 1906 the college became a state institution; it went coeducational in 1918. Its student body, which now numbers approximately 7,500, comes from all over the world. The College of William and Mary is today considered one of the leading educational facilities in this country.

The south wing houses the chapel. Built in 1732, its rich paneling is made of native walnut and pine. Two generations of Randolphs, Lord Botetourt, and Bishop James Madison are buried in the crypt.

The Great Hall was part of the original building and was used to accommodate large meetings, lectures, and balls; it was also the place where the masters, ushers, and students took their meals. While Virginia's new Capitol building was under construction, the House of Burgesses and General Court often convened in this room. It was used again after the Capitol building burned in 1747.

Public recitals are still played on the 1760 organ, located in the gallery where the royal coat of arms of both George I and George II is also displayed.

The Blue Room was used for meetings.

The Grammar School classroom; here students were instructed in academic studies as well as catechism of the Church of England. The enclosed boxes are where ushers would sit to monitor the student benches.

President's House
College of William and Mary

Located on the north side of the college yard in front of the Wren Building is the Georgian-style brick President's House. Like the Wren Building, its restoration was a priority during the re-creation of Williamsburg in 1928. This was, and is still today, the oldest college president's house to exist in the United States. Constructed in 1732-33, this charming home has received many celebrities and seen many changes, both in its architecture and its customs.

All of the early college presidents were religious men, dedicated to serving their King and his colony. Later, while still religious in conviction, the college's presidents owed their allegiance to the needs and fertile minds of a new, independent America. Through all the turmoil in William and Mary's history, however, the college's presidents have used this house—except for one short time.

In 1781, Bishop Madison evacuated the premises to allow British General Cornwallis to rest, on his march to Yorktown. Later that year, wounded French officers stayed in the house after helping to defeat the British at the siege of Yorktown. When the house accidentally burned during this period, King Louis XVI reimbursed the college for its damage.

For more than 250 years the President's House has received thousands of famous individuals, including U.S. presidents, foreign heads of state, dignitaries, and royalty.

As changes in the architecture of the college evolved, so the layout of the house changed. In the final restoration the kitchen was incorporated on the ground floor, as modern living demands. At one time there was a porch out front, and even shutters on the windows. Now the restored building reflects the design of its original Georgian-style structure outside, while comfortably accommodating modern living conditions inside. Eighteenth-century colors have been retained with white plaster walls and subtle gray-green painted woodwork. Bricked-up fireplaces were opened and the Victorian mantles have been replaced with earlier Georgian ones. At one time there was talk of moving the President out to a new house and retaining this building as a museum, but it was overruled.

At the time of its restoration, this "commodious Georgian brick house," as it was referred to, contained only a few pieces of suitable furniture. A group of donors, Friends of the President's House, contracted Clement E. Conger, who was Curator at the White House in Washington, D.C., to head them in their search for period furniture befitting an official residence. This has resulted in a beautiful collection of period furniture, paintings, and carpets, amongst which are William and Mary, Queen Anne, and Chippendale period pieces.

Unfortunately, the house, which still serves as a private residence for the incumbent president, is not open to the public.

The front elevation of the President's House faces south. This simple but elegant two-story traditional Georgian brick house has exceptionally large windows and door-ways, with twelve-foot-high ceilings throughout the first floor.

The passage has a door at the rear. During warm weather, both the front and back doors could be opened to facilitate extra ventilation by producing a cross breeze. In earlier times this hallway served as a waiting room.

Paintings of King William and Queen Mary show the young monarchs soon after their coronation, following the Glorious Revolution in England. These magnificent oils were painted either by Sir Godfrey Kneller (1646-1723) or under his direction. Several rare pieces of treasured fine Virginia-made furniture were also found for the house. An English hall table, ca. 1760, is owned by the college. The brass and glass lantern is from the Netherlands. Originally made for candles, these fittings are now electric.

The two parlors occupy the entire east side of the house downstairs and are divided by a wall with an arched doorway. James Blair entertained William Byrd II of Westover in these rooms. Here too Cherokee Chief Ausrenaco, Presidents Jefferson, Madison, and Monroe, and Chief Justice John Marshall have been received, as have many other United States presidents down through the centuries.

The Georgian brass chandeliers date from about 1740, and paintings of the Page family and a picture of the Duchess of York by Sir Peter Lely hang on the walls. Furnishings include a Chippendale open chair, and a William and Mary period walnut chest. An eighteenth-century Scalamandre silk-covered frame settee is located in the north parlor. Reflected in the looking glass is a 1760 Philadelphia clock with Delaware works. An English-made mahogany tea table, ca. 1750, and a Virginia-made eighteenth-century walnut bookcase, as well as other Queen Anne pieces, furnish the south parlor. Wrought iron and brass fire fork items in the fireplace are also eighteenth-century.

This elegant dining room is situated to the left of the front door. Prominent in this room is the oil painting of another leading, colonial citizen, Maria Byrd Carter (1727-45.) The dining table is a recent handmade reproduction. The chandelier above is English cut crystal, ca. 1740, and was found in a mosque in India. A Hepplewhite sideboard, on the far wall, is ca. 1785, complete with its original brasses. A looking glass over the sideboard, adorned with the phoenix, is eighteenth-century English. The rug is a Persian Serapi, from the beginning of this century. Venetian pull-up curtains in red silk and cotton damask add an unusual touch to this room.

Bruton Parish Church
Duke of Gloucester Street

Originally a parish church was completed on this site in 1683, after several smaller parishes around the community of Middle Plantation were combined into Bruton Parish. This small Flemish-style church then fell into disrepair. Since, furthermore, it could not accomodate the growing population and large number of visitors coming to Williamsburg when the courts convened, it was decided to build a new place of worship befitting the new capital.

The present Bruton Parish Church was constructed in 1712-15. Lieutenant Governor Alexander Spotwood supplied a "draught," or plan, of the building, and the assembly contributed two hundred pounds toward the cost of its construction. Carpenter James Morris supervised the work and Lewis Delony made the pews. The chancel was extended in 1752, and an organ, which came from England, was installed in 1755. A new tower and steeple were added in 1769 and merchant James Tarpley donated a bell, which still rings out today. Virginia supported the early Anglican church, and those who did not attend services could be fined under colonial and early state laws.

During the rectorship of Dr. W. A. R. Goodwin, from 1903 to 1907, the church was returned to its former eighteenth-century appearance. Rev. Goodwin was later instrumental in persuading John D. Rockefeller, Jr., to become financially involved with the reconstruction and restoration of Williamsburg. The building underwent further restoration in 1938-39, with additional modifications in 1940-42. The church, which has been in continuous use since 1715, now holds Episcopal services throughout the year on Sundays and holy days.

Bruton Parish Church viewed from Duke of Gloucester Street. Sections of the original churchyard wall, completed in 1754, still stand today.

The nave and chancel, restored to their eighteenth-century appearance.

A magnificent pulpit, skillfully made from hard woods.

Governor's chair.

Macabre tombs in the churchyard. Many of the table tombs were brought from England.

Near this monum

THE
HON.FRANCIS FAUQUIER.ESQ.

Lieutenant Governour and Commander in
Chief of the Colony over which he presided
near ten years much to his own honour and
the ease and satisfaction of the inhabitants.
He was a gentleman of the most amiable dispo-
sition generous just and mild and possessed in
an eminent degree all the social virtues He was
a fellow of the Royal Society and died in his
65th year the 3rd day of March 1768.

*This marble was placed here at the time of the
Restoration of the Church in 1905.
The inscription is taken from the obituary
notice in the Virginia Gazette which also states
that he was buried in the North Isle of Bruton
Parish Church.*

Some privileged and famous people are buried beneath the sanctuary floor.

James Geddy House
Duke of Gloucester Street

Gunsmith James Geddy owned this property and operated a shop here between about 1737 and his death in 1744. An inventory shows the gunsmith's shop to have contained brasswork for guns, a turner's lathe, bullet molds, and founder's tools. In 1760, Geddy's widow, Anne, sold this property to their son James. James, Jr., built this house and continued business here as a silversmith and goldsmith. He sold and repaired jewelry and also repaired watches. James, Jr., became a community leader as well as a member of the Williamsburg common council.

The house today, which is open to visitors, is a good example of upper-middle-class colonial life. A foundry, which is located in the yard behind the house, demonstrates the skill of casting metals, using eighteenth-century methods.

The front of the James Geddy House faces south, onto Duke of Gloucester Street.

In the parlor, a card table is set up for an evening's entertainment. In winter, a fire would have been lit and a carpet laid upon the bare floor to add comfort.

This room now serves as an interpretation room and has examples of items important in day-to-day colonial living, as well as fine furniture.

A bedroom, with a cradle before the fireplace, shows an aspect of the life that more prosperous craftsmen and their families led.

In the foundry, located behind the house, a craftsman demonstrates turning a bronze candlestick using a treadle lathe.

Courthouse
Market Square

The Courthouse was built facing Market Square in 1770-71. This courthouse was used by two court systems. One was the James City County Court, and the other was known as the Hustings Court for the city of Williamsburg. County courts were responsible for local government, and they held executive and judicial powers, but they were not responsible for cases carrying the death penalty for white offenders. Felonies involving white defendants were heard by the General Court which convened twice a year at the Capitol, although the local courts heard such cases against slaves.

Located halfway along Duke of Gloucester Street, in an area of concentrated activity that includes busy Market Square, the Magazine, and nearby Chowning's Tavern, the Courthouse was no doubt a gathering place to hear important news. It was here that on July 25, 1776, Benjamin Waller, speaking from the courthouse steps, proclaimed the Declaration of Independence to a large crowd after word had arrived from Philadelphia.

The Courthouse's south elevation with its cantilevered portico and impressive octagonal cupola looks out onto Market Square.

The courtroom, where two courts were held: the James City County Court and a municipal court known as the Hustings Court.

Confined in this room without food or sanitation, juries deliberated a defendant's fate by verdict.

The Clerk of the Court, a most important officer of the court, had his own office.

Ominous manacles on the Clerk's office floor.

Chambers for the magistrates' use, or other conferences.

Magazine and Guardhouse
Market Square

Governor Alexander Spotswood ordered the construction of a substantial brick building to hold arms and ammunition sent from England, so this unusual but strong octagon-shaped Magazine was built on Market Square in 1715. Later, during the French and Indian War of 1754-63, a high wall was erected around the building for further protection, and a guardhouse was added nearby.

As unrest in the colony spread, the British government ordered the royal governors to seize stores of weapons and ammunition. Governor Dunmore ordered British marines to remove the gunpowder stored in the Magazine. His command was carried out under cover of darkness, on the night of April 20-1, 1775. Alarmed citizens gathered on Market Square, where town leaders convinced the crowd to send a delegation to the Governor's Palace rather than resort to violence. When Patrick Henry heard the news several days later, he led a group of armed volunteers from Hanover County to reclaim the powder. After British officials made financial restitution to the "rebels," Henry's men dispersed peacefully, leaving their intended prize unclaimed.

Confederate forces stored their powder in the Magazine during the Civil War, and afterwards the building was utilized for many things including a market, a Baptist meeting house, a dance school, and a livery stable. Later the Association for the Preservation of Virginia Antiquities took it under its care. Although Colonial Williamsburg restored the Magazine in 1934-35, the Foundation did not acquire the property from the A.P.V.A. until 1986.

Sheep in pens graze in Market Square before the Magazine, which is surrounded by a high wall.

At left: Magazine guard.

At right: Arms display inside.

Below: Tent-making in the Magazine yard.

The nearby Guardhouse.

Guardroom with militia arms at the ready.

Reenactment by militia men on a green behind the Courthouse.

A school group drilling under the care of a militia man.

In the Military Encampment (open seasonally), a cannon is fired.

Wetherburn's Tavern
Duke of Gloucester Street

Wetherburn's Tavern was built in two sections: the first dates from about 1738, and the second part was probably completed shortly after 1750. In colonial times this tavern was always full of lively activity. Weary travelers rested here overnight; visiting businessmen and officials sometimes stayed a little longer. Local people used the tavern as a place of entertainment where dancing, eating, and drinking, or perhaps a game of cards or dice, went on into the night. Busy with their meetings, lectures, and gatherings, men of science and politics became engrossed in deep conversation within these walls. As Wetherburn's Tavern's popularity grew, it became a major part of Williamsburg social life.

After owner Henry Wetherburn died in 1760, a detailed inventory of the tavern was taken. Deeds and accounts also document his time here. From information written in these records and subsequent items excavated on the property, an accurate reproduction of this colonial tavern and the life centered on it has been constructed for visitors to see.

This large building with its two front doors and many dormer windows faces Williamsburg's main street. The tavern's exterior is painted with a faux whitewash effect, white over dark painted wood, to replicate finishes of the period.

In the public dining room, a cupboard contains antiques that match artifacts discovered when excavations were carried out behind the tavern. Over two hundred thousand fragments of pottery, glass, and metal objects were found during archaeological digs carried out on this site between 1964 and 1966.

Behind is Mr. Wetherburn's small office.

The Great Room was an addition made to the tavern in the early 1750s. A public dining room, this space was also used for large private dinner parties. Dances were held here, and Mr. Wetherburn would sell tickets at the door. The painting of Europa and the Bull in this room represents a scene from classical mythology. The recent excavations at the Roman site of Pompeii fueled the widespread popularity of neoclassical style.

Queen's ware soup tureens are a very elegant type of tableware not usually found in taverns. They are shown here as an example of Mr. Wetherburn's success.

A white marble fireplace is thought to be an original feature.

BELOW: *The Bull Head Room is handsomely furnished and could be rented as a private room for meeting or parties. The combined desk and bookcase contains silverware to illustrate that Mr. Wetherburn's inventory listed a large amount of silver. The tall case clock displayed is American, ca. 1740-70, made in Germantown, Pennsylvania, by Augustine Neisser. Its cabinet is mostly made of walnut with secondary woods of tulip pine and white pine.*

A small bedroom behind the Bull Head Room is a family chamber and might have been used when the tavern was full. Here, a bed with an early trundle bed beneath is where Wetherburn's two daughters would have slept. A row of chairs divides what was the original room from its later addition. A wall support and ceiling beam are further evidence of this alteration.

Large public sleeping spaces upstairs would accommodate several simple beds. Tavern business was regulated by the courts, which established the prices charged for certain goods and services. Regardless of status, if a traveler wanted to economize, this is where he would have slept. The price, however, did not entitle guests to a whole bed to themselves—only a space in a bed.

The leather cases or trunks are portmanteaus, an eighteenth-century version of a suitcase. These could be hooked over a saddle; some were made to be carried. Important travel items, such as a folding candlestick with its own flint and striker, could be purchased from stores in Williamsburg by travellers setting off for the frontier.

BELOW: *Additional public sleeping space includes this passageway upstairs with dormer windows. A row of chamber pots demonstrates how important these vessels were in a busy tavern serving lots of drinks with only an outside privy. The bed is covered with a bed rug made by a Colonial Williamsburg weaver.*

In contrast is this private bedroom with a comfortable four-poster bed. For this accommodation a guest might be charged according to the cut of his clothing and quality of horse he rode. Room service was available here both day and night for those who paid extra. This room could be shared by three people but they didn't necessarily have to be acquainted. In such circumstances the bed with bed hangings would be an obvious advantage, providing privacy as well as warmth in winter.

A typical private sleeping space that could be shared by two or three burgesses who were friends. By requesting to share this room, they would be certain of their privacy and would be able to continue unfinished conversations, left over from a day at the Capitol or important meetings downstairs, late into the night.

An outside kitchen where tavern meals were prepared. A loft area above housed tavern slaves as well as visiting slaves who accompanied their masters.

The large earthenware jar, which originally contained oil from the Mediterranean, was utilized for storage. An archaeological dig on another site in town unearthed jars similar to this one.

Outbuildings contained a kitchen, smokehouse, laundry, dairy, and well. The dairy was the only one to
survive with its original framing. The remainder were
reconstructed on sites revealed in archaeological
excavations. Work buildings were constructed away
from the main tavern because of their heat, smell, and
risk of fire and to separate enslaved workers from genteel clientele.

Raleigh Tavern
Duke of Gloucester Street

Since the Raleigh Tavern's opening around 1717, it has played a significant role in the political history not only of Williamsburg, but also the colony of Virginia and the American Revolution. In 1769, a group of burgesses met in the tavern's Apollo Room and adopted a proposal by George Mason to boycott British goods. This was in retaliation for the dissolution of Virginia's General Assembly, which in turn was a response to the assembly's objection to a new British revenue tax on the colony.

Five years later, the burgesses again met in the Apollo Room and called for a Continental Congress. These events eventually led to the Revolution.

Famous colonial figures could be seen at the tavern regularly. George Washington dined on many occasions and Thomas Jefferson danced here as a young man. Peyton Randolph was entertained at the Raleigh when he returned from Philadelphia, and Patrick Henry was given a farewell dinner by his troops within these walls. Much later, in 1824, a banquet was given for General Lafayette in the Apollo Room.

During the colonial period, the Raleigh Tavern was a busy center of social and political life. Lectures, meetings, auctions, and exhibitions were all held

The public dining room. The kitchen is just outside.

This is the Club Room, one of many entertainment spaces. The tavern is depicted here at night. It would have been a place where gentlemen gathered to discuss politics or travellers exchanged their news.

here. Dinners and balls were commonplace. All manner of items could be bought and sold at the tavern, including merchandise, property, and even slaves. Planters, merchants, and shippers mixed with lawyers, politicians, and aristocrats, all enthusiastically sharing their news, as well as the tavern's excellent food and drink. It was a noisy place, where revelries would continue into the night.

Early accounts and an inventory for the Raleigh have been recovered and have proved invaluable in accurately reconstructing the building and furnishing its rooms. The inventory was used as a guide for the collection of English and American-made furnishings, as well as other significant items, that are on show to the public.

Tucked in the back of the dining room, this tiny apartment is the bar-keeper's bedroom. It is probably where the tavern-keeper originally lived.

Most of the ground-floor rooms were used as dining rooms on occasions. This is the Bar, next to the Club Room, which was available for private or family use.

In contrast, the Apollo Room is huge. Its fame comes from its political history; burgesses met here when the General Assembly had been dissolved. Originally this was copied from a room in London, which still exists today. Bricks in the fireplace are from the old building's foundation and give a hint of floor height.

The Daphne Room, with its ornate marble mantle, is a private dining room behind the Apollo Room. Set up with punch bowls and glasses, it is typical of a space used for small gatherings and receptions.

The Billiards Room would have been popular and perhaps the noisiest part of the building. Located at the rear, it overlooks a yard where a kitchen, laundry, and servant's quarters are located.

Also located in the rear yard and very popular with visitors is a Bake Shop. Here fresh bread, cakes, and rolls are sold every day. A large hearth displays colonial-period bakery tools, baskets, and products. A variety of jarred and packaged goods are also for sale.

Upstairs

More lodging space. At this moment, the tavern appears very quiet, but two hundred years ago this would have been a lively, noisy place, especially with gentlemen coming to discuss politics and play friendly card games, or just to find out what was going on at the tavern. The bar was open all hours until the last drinker had gone to bed. With all its rowdiness, it would have been a problem getting a good night's sleep here.

A lodging space is set up with an artist's easel to demonstrate that painters traveled throughout the colony.

A tavern-keeper was required by law to provide food, drink, and lodging for a man, his horse, and his slave. This lodging space is depicted with models of a traveller in bed and a slave accommodated at the foot of the bed.

Capitol
eastern end of Duke of Gloucester Street

Built in an unusual two-story, H-shaped configuration with round fronted wings and entrances on either side of an impressive piazza, this imposing brick building stands within its own walled yard. Construction of the original Capitol was started in 1701. Eager to vacate their earlier meeting place at the College of William and Mary, lawmakers moved into this building in 1704, one year before it was actually completed.

Virginia's new seat of government housed the Council and General Court on one side and the House of Burgesses on the other. For eighty-one years Williamsburg was the Virginia Colony's political center and much of its legislation was determined within these walls. Patrick Henry made his famous "Caesar-Brutus" speech of 1765 on this site. The 1776 Resolution for Independence was adopted here and Thomas Jefferson's bill for religious freedom was proposed here. The General Court, the colony's highest court, was convened in the Capitol building. Twice a year serious cases would be tried and convicted offenders dispatched for punishment, which could be either branding or a whipping at the town pillory—or hanging.

South elevation of the Capitol, showing its unique round fronted wings.

The first Capitol building burned down in 1747, and a second was completed in its place six years later. In 1780, Virginia's government moved the capital to Richmond. Neglected like many public buildings in Williamsburg, the Capitol fell into disrepair and later burned down.

As part of the plan to revitalize Williamsburg, it was decided to reconstruct the first Capitol building on its original foundations and then furnish it according to surviving architectural information.

Capitol entrance lit by lanterns at night.

Hall of the House of Burgesses.

General Court, where legislation was approved and justices held the High Court of Appeals for both civil and criminal cases.

The second floor's west wing contains the Council Chamber, where the upper house of the General Assembly, the Council, convened. The table, which is covered with a wool carpet authentic to the time, bears a Bible known as the Vinegar Bible. This name refers to a sub-heading in a passage from the gospel of St. Luke, where the word "vineyard" is misprinted.

Filled with portraits of the country's leading founding fathers, this Conference Room spans the second floor over the piazza, forming a symbolic bridge between the Council and the House of Burgesses.

One of several committee rooms where burgesses met to talk over proposed legislation.

Clerks and secretaries had smaller offices at the rear.

AT LEFT: *The impressive stairway on the west side of the building is decorated with a faux marble design.*

65

Bassett Hall
Francis Street

The Williamsburg home of Mr. and Mrs. John D. Rockefeller, Jr., Bassett Hall was built between 1753 and 1766. It was modified considerably over the years. It is believed that this wood-frame house, a two-story dwelling, was constructed by Colonel Philip Johnson, a member of the House of Burgesses. A one and one-half story wing was added at the back of the house. Today, the eighteenth-century front portion consists of two rooms downstairs and two rooms upstairs. The dining room area in the back was enlarged in this century. A caretaker's wing was also added and the interior was converted for modern living. In this respect it is different from other period houses on show in the Historic Area, as it has a modern kitchen and bathrooms.

Bassett Hall gets its name from long-time owner Burwell Bassett, who bought the property in about 1800. He was the nephew of Martha Washington and a congressman, state senator, and delegate.

John D. Rockefeller, Jr., and his wife, Abby Aldrich, moved into Bassett Hall in 1936. The 585-acre estate provided them with a residence when visiting

Bassett Hall's north elevation looks out onto pristine lawns, a long driveway, and, in the distance, the Capitol.

Williamsburg to oversee the reconstruction of buildings. Here the philanthropist would meet with the Reverend Dr. W. A. R. Goodwin, the originator of the idea to restore Williamsburg, and together they would discuss its transformation.

Abby Aldrich Rockefeller, whose donation of more than four hundred pieces of folk art from her personal collection formed the nucleus of the Abby Aldrich Rockefeller Folk Art Center in Williamsburg, brought many of the family's familiar and favorite pieces from other homes throughout the country. This resulted in a marvellous, eclectic collection of fine porcelain, pictures, rugs, and antique furniture, juxtaposed with high quality American folk art. All of this has remained virtually undisturbed since the family lived here, and the public is able to see how the Rockefellers and their children lived amongst and with the pieces of this premier and cherished collection.

The Rockefeller family left Bassett Hall and its contents to the Colonial Williamsburg Foundation in 1979. This delightful house is open to the public. There is also a nature trail to explore on the extensive grounds.

In the hallway, or "passage," is the original eighteenth-century staircase. Some panels were charred in a fire in 1930, when the floor above was destroyed. The tall case mahogany clock is by William Robinson of London, ca. 1800.

The Morning Room was the Rockefellers' favorite gathering place when they were in residence. Some of the more unusual pieces here are Turkish Kula prayer rugs; a variety of English porcelain figures and dishes; and a selection of chalkware ornaments. Mrs. Rockefeller's interest in folk art is evident in the paintings on the walls and two needlework pictures on either side of the fireplace. One of her most important finds, displayed over the desk, was a portrait of *Child Posing with Cat, the six-teenth portrait attributed to the yet-to-be-identified New England artist known to scholars as the Beardsley Limner. It was painted about 1790.*

This formal parlor was used on more elegant occasions. The room is centered on a nineteenth-century French Aubusson carpet. Needlework pictures in this room were done by young ladies who attended fashionable schools. They were expected to develop needlework skills in addition to their academic studies.

One of a pair of Chinese export porcelain hawks. Dated between 1720 and 1760, these are considered to be among the finest ceramics here at Bassett Hall because of their age and artistry.

The large elegant dining room has a cock weather-vane looking down from the unusually high mantle, which is also decorated with pastel portraits attributed to Charles Hayter and a bust painted by Félice Cornè.

In the upstairs hall, this intricately carved chest was made by Mrs. Rockefeller's brother, Stuart Aldrich. His hobby was wood carving and he gave this piece to Mr. and Mrs. Rockefeller as a wedding gift.

The master bedroom is centered on the unusually large twist-hooked rug, which was purchased from the grandson of its maker. Most of the paintings in this room are stenciled works called theorem paintings—another example of folk art.

The Rockefellers enjoyed collecting figurines that represent the four seasons. On the mantle is one of three sets of lusterware in the house.

A guest bedroom. Like the master bedroom, this room is decorated with theorem paintings.

Williamsburg Inn
Francis Street

A distinguished five-star hotel, the Williamsburg Inn is modeled after a nineteenth-century West Virginia spa hotel building, faced in white brick. Interior decor is reminiscent of the Regency period. Facilities include restaurants serving excellent cuisine and beautifully appointed rooms overlooking terraces and splendid golf courses. Additional recreation includes two swimming pools, tennis, and lawn bowls. Located on a secluded site adjacent to the Historic Area, the inn is but a short walk from Duke of Gloucester Street.

Columns support the building's portico over the front entrance to this distinguished hotel.

White-washed brick exterior secluded in trees—

—overlooks magnificent golfing facilities.

The Regency Room, renowned for its cuisine.

An elegant lobby with fireplaces at each end.

The upper dining room of the Williamsburg Inn overlooks one of the golf courses.

Antique tall case clock located in the hallway.

AT LEFT: *Comfortable guest rooms, tastefully furnished
to capture period lifestyle.*

Lightfoot House
Francis Street

This Georgian house, decorated with bricks laid in the Flemish bond pattern and an ornate outer garden fence made in Chinese Chippendale style, dates from about 1730; it was altered to its current form in the mid-1700s. Surprisingly, architectural evidence suggests it functioned as a "tenement," or rental property, and embraced several living units. Other notable features of this particularly grand house are its second floor level, which is equal in height to the first floor, and unusually high windows and a wrought iron balcony over the front door, similar to the Governor's Palace. Elegant residences like this were usually built for a wealthy family. Colonel Philip Lightfoot, who owned this beautiful mansion in the late eighteenth century, was indeed a wealthy merchant and planter.

The house, which had many private owners through its two-century history, was taken over by the Colonial Williamsburg Foundation in 1961 and restored as accommodations for special guests and visiting dignitaries. Several wood-frame cottages in the rear garden were also reconstructed, and these are used for additional accommodations.

Front elevation of the Lightfoot House, a splendid Georgian-style mansion that was divided into several distinct living units.

Of particular note, a Chinese-influenced Chippendale design garden fence is based on a fashionable pattern of the eighteenth century.

BELOW: *Overlooking the parlor is an oil portrait of Mary Churchill, Duchess of Montagu, from the school of Sir Godfrey Kneller. Other furnishings include a French looking glass with gold gesso frame, ca. 1643-1715, and an English sofa from between 1760 and 1775. A mahogany breakfront, English, ca. 1775, contains a collection of Worcester porcelain. An eighteenth-century Chinese panel black coffee table stands on the Oriental Joshagan rug.*

The elegant dining room is decorated with hand-painted wallpaper in a Chinese design. A japanned framed Queen Anne looking glass hangs over the mahogany side table with a marble top, ca. 1720-35. An English cut glass chandelier, ca. 1760, hangs above the three-pedestal dining table which is surrounded by chairs of walnut with seat covers in copper silk damask, English, ca. 1730. An exquisite pair of eighteenth-century Italian japanned corner cabinets with engraved mirrored glass doors fills the corners.

This bedroom where kings and queens have slept centers on twin tall post beds with bed hangings in reproduction fabric made by F. Schumacher & Co. for Colonial Williamsburg. Between the beds is an early eighteenth-century framed embroidered chenille needlework panel on silk taffeta. An English-made mahogany desk with brass handles, ca. 1740, is accompanied by an upholstered George II chair and backstool in mahogany, both English, ca. 1750.

A second bedroom features a large four-poster bed with matching gold damask tester, head curtains, and bed cover. Furnishings include Hepplewhite fruit-wood chairs and an Oxbow front secretary desk, ca. 1790.

At the top of the stairs in the second-floor hall is a cupboard by Kittinger, full of antique Chinese export Delft and English Worcester porcelain.

Abby Aldrich Rockefeller Folk Art Center
South England Street

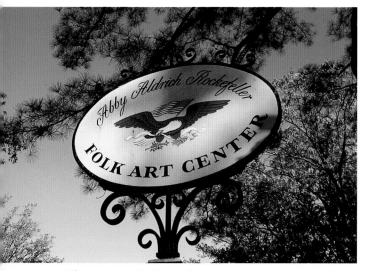

The museum's sign at its gateway.

This museum, which opened in 1957, started with a personal folk art collection given by Abby Aldrich Rockefeller to Colonial Williamsburg in 1939. In 1988-91, the museum was enlarged to house the growing collection. Galleries located on three floors show paintings, sculptures, toys, furniture, decor, pottery, quilts, and other objects. All are attributed to ordinary people, hence the name "folk," but the variety and imagination of the untrained artists are both enlightening and inspiring.

Open daily by ticketed admission, the museum also has an excellent gift shop.

BELOW: *Front elevation of the 1957 building which houses the Abby Aldrich Rockefeller Folk Art Center.*

The World Made Small, a popular Christmas exhibit of antique toys and miniatures.

A Christmas tree decorates the entrance to the Folk Art in American Life Gallery.

The Sculpture Gallery exhibits American folk art mostly carved from wood.

DeWitt Wallace Gallery
Francis Street

The DeWitt Wallace Gallery is a modern museum to which access is gained through the main entrance of the Public Hospital building.

Named for its benefactor, DeWitt Wallace, who was the founder of *Reader's Digest,* this 62,000-square-foot museum was designed by architect Kevin Roche. An impressive collection of seventeenth-century to early-nineteenth-century English and American decorative arts includes items of furniture, silver, ceramics, paintings, textiles, and domestic objects, all displayed in galleries located on two floors.

A central stairway with courtyard and balcony gives visitors access to both exhibition levels.

Furniture displayed in one of the many fine galleries.

Orchids and other tropical plants adorn a restful courtyard garden inside the museum.

Public Hospital
Francis Street

The building of the continent's first hospital devoted solely to mental health was completed in 1773. In the beginning this institution employed primitive remedies including restraints, drugs, bleeding, plunge baths, and confinement in cells with barred windows. Patients were attended by a doctor, usually once a week, but for the most part were left in the care of James Galt and his wife. Galt had previously been "gaoler" at the Public Gaol.

Improvements were made in the treatment of mental patients in the century that followed, however. The building was enlarged and additional structures were built to accommodate in excess of four hundred chronically ill people. In 1885, a fire completely destroyed the original building.

As part of the reconstruction of Colonial Williamsburg this impressive building was erected along the lines of the original hospital. Open as a museum, inside it visitors can experience life as it was in an eighteenth-century cell, then see the contrast with a patient's apartment from one hundred years later. Interpretive displays with audio accompaniment add reality to the exhibit.

The Public Hospital lobby also gives access to the DeWitt Wallace Gallery, which contains the most impressive collection of colonial artifacts anywhere.

North elevation of the Public Hospital facing Francis Street.

Primitive cell of the 1773 era.

More comfortable mid-1800s accommodation for the insane.

George Wythe House
Palace Street

The main house on this extra-large in-town property is an original Georgian-style brick building which dates from about 1750. George Wythe probably moved into this home in 1755 when he married Elizabeth Taliaferro. It was originally built and owned by Elizabeth's father; Taliaferro willed his daughter and her bridegroom lifetime rights to live in the house upon his death in 1775.

George Wythe was born on a plantation about thirty miles southeast of Williamsburg, near Hampton, Virginia. During his lifetime he had quite a celebrated career. He served as the mayor of Williamsburg, was elected to the House of Burgesses, and was a delegate to both the Continental Congress and the Constitutional Convention. He signed the Declaration of Independence. He was also on the Board of Visitors at the college of William and Mary. Wythe taught law privately and later at William and Mary; at the college, he had the distinction of being the first person to hold a chair of law in an American university. Wythe's law students included Thomas Jefferson, John

The imposing Georgian-style George Wythe House on Palace Street. George Washington used the premises as his headquarters preceding the siege of Yorktown. French Commander Rochambeau took over the house in 1781 while resting his troops in Williamsburg after Cornwallis surrendered.

Marshall, and Henry Clay. Jefferson called Wythe his mentor and lifelong friend. Wythe also tutored in other subjects, including Greek, Latin, and French, as well as English literature and mathematics. At the time of his suspicious death in 1806 at age eighty, he was studying Hebrew.

George Wythe's life probably ended as a result of poisoning. It was thought but never proven that the poison was administered by his grandnephew George Sweeney, who had been the principal beneficiary of his will. Although Sweeney was never convicted, Wythe lived long enough to disinherit him.

With the exception of the house, buildings on the lot have been reconstructed on their original sites as determined by archaeologists. These include a kitchen, laundry, lumber house used for storage, poultry house, well, dove cote, and stable with carriage house attached. All the work in these outbuildings was done by slaves and this is possibly where they lived. George Wythe had between twelve and eighteen slaves at one point, but felt very uncomfortable with slavery and thought it was wrong. When his wife died he gave most of his slaves to his wife's family. Later on he freed the remainder except for three, including a female named Lydia Broadnax, who was his cook, and a male slave who was probably her husband (slaves were not usually allowed to marry, but they could have an informal wedding ceremony). All three were later freed when he moved to Richmond, but he took them with him as freemen and presumably paid them.

The gardens are planted with vegetables and herbs, just as they were in the eighteenth century. Herbs were used as an important source of medication as well as for cooking. The formal garden with its carefully tended borders and boxwood hedges is particularly elegant.

This distinctive bright blue passage wallpaper was reproduced from the original two-hundred-year-old printing blocks owned by the manufacturer in England.

In the master bedroom is a four-poster bed and furnishings with accurately reproduced fabric depicting George Washington being honored by Native Americans. The original fabric, which is historically significant, is stored to protect it from damaging light and climatic conditions.

A downstairs bedroom with attractive red wool bed hangings is a lady's room where the occupant could write letters at the splendid desk or do needlework by window light.

The well-appointed dining room downstairs has framed engravings covering its walls. Quality porcelain and glassware indicate a family of some position in colonial society.

Red damask wallpaper and a carpet add to the parlor's comfort. Six color prints of flower arrangements hang over the mantle and fine porcelain is kept in a corner cabinet.

In his role as educator, George Wythe undertook scientific experiments and this involvement grew well beyond mere interest. Depicted in his office is scientific equipment of the period.

An upstairs "lumber" room stores an unfinished quilt on a frame. On occasion a slave may have stayed in this room to be close to Mrs. Wythe, who was in failing health for several years.

In the kitchen, a cook demonstrates a small copper pot being used to cook a stew with charcoal from the fireplace. The large oven would have been fired up only for baking bread, because it took many hours and much wood.

Slave quarters are attached to the kitchen.

The stables adjoin . . .

. . . the coach house.

A dove cote in the rear yard.

Vegetables and herbs were an important part of any colonial garden.

The Governor's Palace

When the Governor's Palace was completed in 1722, it was hailed as one of the finest buildings in British America. This remarkable structure was started in 1706 after the General Assembly voted to build a residence for the royal governor, Edward Nott, and appropriated three thousand pounds toward its construction. Work went slowly at first and by the time Alexander Spotswood became governor in 1710, the Palace was still only a shell. He insisted the building be completed and proposed new legislation to appropriate further funds. As a result, extraordinary extravagance was lavished upon both the interior and exterior of the building, as well as its surrounding sixty-three-acre estate, which included woodlands, meadows, ornamental gardens, and terraces that reach down to an enclosed canal. At a time when most dwellings were very simple in their construction, the imposing location and impressive proportions of this architectural wonder were obviously intended to implant a healthy amount of respect for the ruling authority among the people.

The imposing front elevation of the Governor's Palace with its surrounding brick wall. Cannons guard the entrance gate.

The lion and the unicorn, symbols of British rule, above white painted wrought iron gates.

Inside, the entrance hall ceiling, walls, and stairway were decorated with weaponry, in what some described as the "ingenious contrivance" of Colonel Spotswood. Contemporaries noted that Spotswood had "rendered the House Convenient as well as Ornamental." Although he had moved into the Palace by 1716, this flamboyant royal governor continued to make improvements and alterations until the Assembly complained about the intolerable cost of his extravagances. Upset by this criticism Spotswood refused to associate himself with further improvements to the building or its grounds.

By the time Lieutenant Governor Robert Dinwiddie arrived in 1751, the building was in a deteriorated state, but repairs soon made the Governor's Palace fit for occupation. Greater changes took place in the following months as plans to expand and embellish the building were put into operation. Mimicking England's preference for adding large, highly visible entertaining spaces to prominent buildings, a rear wing including a fashionable ballroom with enormous high windows and a supper room was added.

In this new luxurious environment, powerful and influential colonial dignitaries were entertained. As splendid as these occasions must have been, the positive impression created by them was overcome by taxation. With the advent of the Stamp Act, colonists started on the road to rebellion. Eventually, John Murray, fourth Earl of Dunmore, Virginia's last royal governor, fled Williamsburg in the early days of the American Revolution. After independence was declared, Patrick Henry became the Commonwealth of Virginia's first governor and took up residence in the palace. Thomas Jefferson also lived here when he later became governor.

Virginia's capital was transferred to Richmond in 1780 and the Palace was vacated. Following the siege of Yorktown in 1781, the building became a makeshift hospital; many American soldiers died here and were buried in the garden. Finally, in an unbefitting end, a fire completely destroyed the palace building in 1781.

The reconstructed Governor's Palace we see today is one of the major achievements in the re-creation of Colonial Williamsburg. With the help of research and many old records, the palace has been rebuilt exactly on its original site. Particular attention was paid to refinements both in architectural detail and decorative features. Every effort was made to recapture its original splendor.

A peaceful ornamental canal in the Palace gardens.

The decor of the Governor's Palace entrance hall was Alexander Spotswood's way of impressing visitors to the Palace with his power as representative of the British crown. Muskets, sabers, and pistols make a decorative circular ceiling pattern and also cover the paneled walls here and throughout the stairwell.

Weaponry decorates the paneled staircase.

To the right of the front door is this parlor, which also served as a waiting room where most people were received. Only important visitors went beyond.

The butler's pantry with its glassware. This room was also conveniently located just inside the front door.

Furnished with personal effects, the governor's dining room was downstairs. Because this area was cool, he did much of his work here. On the mantle shelf is an original commemorative set of Chelsea porcelain figures in masquerade costume, made in honor of King George III's twenty-first birthday party. The map is by Patrick Henry's father John Henry, made before Patrick was governor.

The ballroom, considered to be one of the grandest rooms in Williamsburg, where upper-class Virginians would be invited on special occasions. Here hang life-sized oil portraits of King George III and Queen Charlotte. As many as thirty couples would attend balls held to celebrate royal birthdays and other important events. After their introduction to the governor, guests would dance the steps of the minuet, accompanied by a quartet.

A Buzalo coal-burning stove was imperative in winter in such a large room. The original is in the Wallace Gallery.

When dancing was over guests would adjourn to this supper room beyond the ballroom. Here too are examples of crafted wood moldings and carved door pediments. Of particular note are the early linen spring shades on the windows. Both the chamber organ and bureau organ are examples of period musical instruments.

A Yuletide table in the supper room.

A comfortably carpeted library used by the governor as an office.

Upstairs is a reception room which has a gilded hand-tooled leather wall-covering similar to the original. This particular leather was found in a manor home in England. Fashionable red checked slip covers made of linen were used to protect the chairs' silk fabric. These would have been removed for formal occasions.

Under the four-poster bed is a Wilton carpet called a bed round. This bedroom was used as a guest room by some of the governors.

A four-poster bed with elaborate design atop. This was the height of fashion in 1768. Governors from other colonies might have stayed in this bedroom.

BELOW: *Romantic white bed curtains and soft green wood-paneled walls. The colors are accurate; green and purple were very popular. Thomas Chippendale, the famous furniture maker, wrote in his directory that green was a color both fashionable and desirable for one's home. Oriental designs greatly influenced this period and are represented here by reproduction rococo chairs, painted in a bamboo pattern. These were copied from one original chair from England and have been placed in two bedrooms to illustrate the style's popularity.*

In the Palace yard are the kitchen and . . .

. . . storeroom.

Scullery and kitchen.

Down in the wine cellars, bottles hold the vintage.

Rear view of the Governor's Palace from a garden with sculptured boxwood hedges.

Close-up of the royal coat of arms over the rear entrance.

The Wheelright is located in the Palace yard. Even today, wheels are made here for carriages that give rides to Colonial Williamsburg visitors.

A carriage house is located nearby.

Symbol of sovereignty, decorative ironwork topped by a gold painted crown, over the Palace courtyard's front gate.

Brush-Everard House
Palace Street

John Brush built this timber-framed house about 1718-20. A local armorer and gunsmith, Brush was also employed as the first keeper of Williamsburg's Magazine, which is located on Market Square. The original one and one-half story dwelling would have been much simpler than the house we see today. Wings on the rear were not there and even the staircase was a later addition. After Brush died, in 1727, the property was lived in by several owners until William Dering purchased it in 1742. A dance master and painter, Dering would have mixed with the local gentry because he taught the elaborate minuet. Fashion demanded that cultured members of polite society be proficient in this dance.

One of the first houses to be built in Williamsburg, the Brush-Everard House faces west onto Palace Street. Starting life as a tradesman's modest dwelling, it was remodeled into a structure befitting its prestigious location near the Governor's Palace.

About 1755, civic leader Thomas Everard moved into this house and stayed for twenty-five years. Everard proceeded to remodel the house, converting it to befit his position in society. He was twice mayor of Williamsburg, deputy clerk of the General Court up until the revolution, and clerk of York County Court for nearly forty years until his death in 1781. He also served on the vestry of Bruton Parish Church.

Early colonial houses were covered with hand-split oak weather boards, and the roofs were of clapboards in place of shingles. Some of these original roofing boards in the Brush-Everard House still exist, protected over the years by a replacement roof. The two wings at the rear may have been added. In keeping with Everard's station in life, some of the interior was paneled and decorated with carvings. The furnishings in this house are from his period. Archaeological excavation on the property revealed original paving, now replicated in the rear yard. Other restoration was also carried out on the out-buildings, which consist of a wooden smokehouse and a brick-built kitchen.

A "chamber," or bedroom, in the north wing at the rear is a gentleman's sleeping quarters. His wife had died by this period, so this was Everard's bed chamber. The wallpaper is a copy of the original paper found here when the house was restored. It would have been hand block printed in England in the eighteenth century. The intense color is based on microscopic analysis of the paints used to color the paper, as are the paint colors on the woodwork throughout the house.

Depicting a family parlor, this room is located on the other side of the back porch. This is where members of the family would have spent their time when not entertaining. Everard might also have conducted his business from this room. He recorded deeds and wills and did some of his work as clerk of York County here at his desk. This particular desk and bookcase was made in Petersburg, Virginia, about 1775.

Just inside the front door are a wide hallway and stairs, possibly added in the second quarter of the eighteenth century. Carved stair brackets, which date from about 1755, are quite similar to those on the grand staircase in the Carter's Grove mansion. The stair carpet is a British Wilton, copied from a surviving eighteenth-century pattern.

This front parlor would have been used for formal entertaining, such as an evening of music and cards. Unlike some other first-floor rooms, it is not wallpapered, although recent research indicates that this color was also used with wallpaper, as were ocher, white, gray, and pink. The piano was made in London, England, in 1746.

Roughly etched into a glass pane of the formal parlor's side window is an inscription that reads, "1796
Oh fatal day." In another pane below, an etching of
a sailing ship is also scratched into the glass and
underneath is signed, "H B Smith Nov 17th 1875."

The dining room is laid out as a room at rest, with its
furniture put back to the walls. Here the wallpaper is
again an exact copy of original paper. A painted floorcloth was considered expedient in an area of high
traffic because it could be wet-mopped.

This second-floor chamber over the parlor was one of two bedrooms used by Everard's daughters, Frances and Martha. They would have been adults in the time period interpreted in this house.

In this bedroom is an eighteenth-century field bed, which was a domestic development from military field camp beds. These were considered useful in rooms with low ceilings, for obvious reasons. The bright blue painted on the trim is again an original color.

Robertson's Windmill
New England Street

This splendid reconstructed post mill stands on land owned in the early eighteenth century by William Robertson. Mills like this could grind up to two hundred pounds of cornmeal an hour when a good wind was blowing. The miller would set his canvas-covered sails, then rotate the mill-house to face into the wind. This started two huge mill stones turning inside. Ground cornmeal and flour were then sifted to separate the meal from the hard shell of the grain and the meal was put into sacks on the lower level. Sometimes people brought their own grain to be ground, paying the miller with a percentage of their grist. Visitors can watch this mill working on windy days and also see demonstrations of rural trades.

This mill is supported and turned on a massive post of hewed wood.

Turning this large wheel positions the mill to face an oncoming wind.

Here a cooper works making his oak barrels.

Weaving baskets is a seasonal farm activity.

Peyton Randolph House
Nicholson Street

Constructed in two sections over about forty years, this imposing two-story white wood-framed house was the home of Peyton Randolph for more than fifty years, from 1721 to 1775. He attended the College of William and Mary, studied law at Inns of Court in London, and shortly thereafter became attorney general of Virginia. Serving in many of the colony's highest governmental offices, including that of Speaker of the House of Burgesses, he later became president of the first and second Continental Congresses. His father, Sir John Randolph, a distinguished lawyer, was the only colonial Virginian to be knighted. When Sir John died in 1737, he bequeathed the house to his widow during her lifetime and thereafter to his son Peyton.

The original dwelling faced North England Street. In 1724 Sir John purchased the adjoining property on Nicholson Street, which included a one and one-half story house. About 1745 a two-story building was constructed to join the two houses together. Unusual for its seven fully paneled rooms, this house features fine furnishings befitting a family of prominent standing in colonial social and political life.

Peyton Randolph was cousin to Thomas Jefferson; upon Peyton's death in 1775, Jefferson purchased his library. Many of these books later became the nucleus of the Library of Congress in Washington, D.C.

The Peyton Randolph House with its green shuttered windows.

The parlor's fine furniture conveys a message of colonial affluence and comfort.

Original family silverware is displayed in the house.

Wall paneling painted in a light color makes these bedrooms very comfortable. Four-poster beds, dressing tables, and numerous chairs furnish these sleeping quarters.

The furniture is composed of original American and English period pieces, representative of the Randolph family's wealth.

The northeast bedroom on the second floor is paneled completely in oak.

The study, with a desk/reading table and book presses.

At the landing dividing the central stairway, a round-topped window overlooks Robertson's Windmill in the distance.

Public Gaol
Nicholson Street

Legislation was passed in 1701 for the construction of a strong, brick-built prison for Williamsburg. In addition to the building, a high wall was built around a yard where prisoners were allowed to exercise. By 1711, overcrowding had made it necessary to construct additional cells, mainly for debtors. Later a connecting brick house was built for the "gaoler" and his family; on the upper floors were rooms for petty offenders. Other prisoners were held in unheated spaces, though provision for sanitation was made in the form of cesspits adjoining each cell. The more seriously accused were sometimes shackled in handcuffs, leg irons, and chains while they waited their turn to go before the General Court.

Exterior of the Public Gaol, showing the 1722 house and the high wall around the exercise yard.

In 1772, an act was passed making creditors solely responsible for their debtors' prison fees. Not wanting more financial liability, fewer creditors pressed charges. This eased pressure both on debtors and on the gaol.

The Public Gaol has held a wide variety of prisoners during its long history. Renegade Indians, pirates, thieves, runaway slaves, forgers, murderers, and debtors have all been locked up here. Even the insane were accommodated within these walls until Williamsburg's Public Hospital was completed in 1773. During the American Revolution, British governor Henry Hamilton, infamous for enticing Indians to scalp Americans, also spent time incarcerated behind these walls. As a military prison, the gaol was used to hold British redcoats, Tory sympathizers, traitors, deserters, and spies.

This building served as Williamsburg's jail in some form up until 1910. Parts of the old gaol's high walls are original. The remainder has been carefully reconstructed. Visitors can go inside both the house and the cells, where the grim horrors of colonial justice can be experienced.

Inside the exercise yard, strong cell doors now stand open for public viewing.

An impregnable window, open to the elements but impossible for a person to pass through.

*A comfortable "hall," the family room of the eighteenth century. This room func-
tioned as the gaoler's office and the family's dining room, parlour, study, and living
room.*

This first-floor bedroom is smaller than any cell but furnished with family comforts.

Benjamin Powell House
Waller Street

Patriot Benjamin Powell lived on this property from 1763 to 1782. He was a general contractor by trade, called an "undertaker" in eighteenth-century colonial Virginia, and constructed many buildings in Williamsburg including the Public Hospital and the tower and steeple of Bruton Parish Church. He also made alterations to the Public Gaol. Together with other prominent citizens, Powell was a member of the committee that put an embargo on British goods in 1774.

The restored house is furnished to represent the surroundings of a rising middle-class family. Activities for school groups and visitors are regularly held in the building and on the grounds. A separate brick building near the house was thought to have been used as an office by a later owner, Dr. Robert Waller, whose family presumably gave the street its name.

The front elevation of the restored Benjamin Powell House faces west. It has two brick chimneys, dormer windows, and a gable roof.

This room with its painted floorcloth was used for dining, but it also doubled as an office. A large fireplace heated this oversized area, which is supported above by a ceiling beam.

Set up here for tea and entertainment, the parlor is where visiting groups now learn about colonial life. The harpsichord was a popular musical instrument.

On the ground floor, a bedroom with its red-checked curtains and chair covers is typical of the period.

Narrow stairs and a long hallway lead from the front door.

Located in an outbuilding, this kitchen is built around a huge fireplace and work space. Drying peppers overhead are from the nearby garden.

A rear view of this fine brick house with its back porch overlooking a yard. Beyond is a vegetable and herb garden used to instruct school groups.

Taverns

   Four historic taverns throughout Colonial Williamsburg are open to the public as restaurants. Each one serves a good selection of hearty colonial-style dishes in congenial, recaptured eighteenth-century surroundings.

Chowning's Tavern, opened in 1766, is located in Duke of Gloucester Street on the corner of Market Square. Josiah Chowning was after the working man's business and therefore kept refinements to a minimum.

One of the dining areas. Specialties include Brunswick stew; Welsh rarebit (please don't call it rabbit), which is melted cheese on toasted bread; bubble and squeak; and shepherd's stew.

Inside, Chowning's displays a rugged appearance with heavy country furniture and booths. Outside dining is available under an arbor in a pleasant garden.

Less than one-half mile east on Williamsburg's main street stand two other eating taverns, the King's Arms and Shields Tavern.

Seeking to attract a more select patronage, the King's Arms Tavern offered more genteel dining. Today a traditional southern menu of peanut soup, Virginia ham, fried chicken, game pie, and Sally Lunn bread is served.

At Left: *Good quality period-style furniture and beautifully paneled walls make dining here a pleasure.*

At Right: *A hall stairway leads to smaller dining areas above.*

The Shields Tavern fare is more robust and will satisfy even the hungriest traveler. Spit-roasted meats, a "sampler" of eighteenth-century recipes, and a sixteenth-century dessert called "Syllabub" can be ordered. Syllabub, or Sillabub as it is sometimes written, is cream, sweetener, and wine folded into a soft curd and then whipped.

Dining in the Shields cellar by candlelight is an unforgettable experience.

Located at the eastern end of Colonial Williamsburg on Waller Street, Christiana Campbell's Tavern serves a variety of dishes found in the thirteen original colonies, including grilled seafood and fried chicken.

The Campbell's Tavern front porch, a good place to argue eighteenth-century politics . . .

. . . with this view of the Capitol through the trees.

Trades of Colonial Williamsburg

In addition to the exhibition buildings in Colonial Williamsburg, there are many trade sites open to visitors. Most of the trades practiced at these sites were an essential part of colonial life and some skilled artisans were not only respected in the community but were also relatively well off. Many people emigrating from the mother country had already learned their skills but, with little room for advancement in a crowded economy at home, had decided that the colonies held a better future for them. In the beginning it was much cheaper and more practical to import many things. As the population grew and towns were established, however, skilled tradespeople found enough affluent clients to support their businesses. During the years leading up to the American Revolution, when several boycotts were put on British goods in retaliation for a series of tax measures, the colony had to rely much more on locally made goods.

In addition to manufactured goods there were also essential personal services performed by people like the milliner, shoemaker, and even the printer. It was just not practical to send to England for a wig, for example, and custom-made carpentry and blacksmithing had to be done by a man on the spot. So colonial Williamsburg became a center of luxury trades and commercial enterprises, creating its own commerce not only with townspeople but also with the growing population on the plantations.

The Post Office on Duke of Gloucester Street heads up a small complex of allied trades which includes printing, bookbinding, and sometimes paper making.

Represented here in Colonial Williamsburg is a cross section of trades carried out during the period. It was usual to work only through the daylight hours, closing shop by nightfall.

Printing Office: A printer applying ink to type.

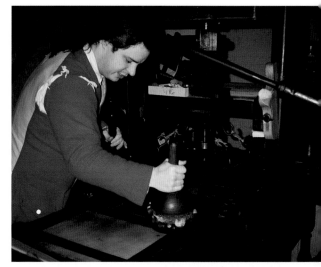

Bookbindery: A bookbinder interprets his craft for visitors.

Costumed interpreters outside the Margaret Hunter Shop, where the milliner plies her trade.

The milliner also sold accessories, games, ceramics, and sewing supplies.

Two of the milliner's employees working on garments.

Although weaving was a domestic, not a trade, activity, there is a loom in operation in a building behind the Margaret Hunter Shop.

The skills of the silversmith and the engraver are demonstrated at the Golden Ball. On the east side of the building, gold and silver jewelry inspired by the colonial era are sold.

James Anderson Blacksmith Shop. Although the blacksmith could make everything from nails to decorative wrought iron for balconies, most of his time was spent repairing wagons and farm tools.

The wigmaker demonstrating the exacting skill required in her occupation.

Shoemaker's Shop. These men would work every daylight hour, hand-stitching and forming leather around a last, custom making footwear.

The harnessmaker-saddler working leather hide into equestrian finery.

A cabinetmaker working on a chair leg by window light.

Hay's Cabinetmaking Shop sits in a gorge with a stream running beneath the building.

Using only hand tools, a carpenter is planing planks of poplar wood.

The carpenter demonstrates his skills at the Carpenter's and Brickmaker's Yard.

The Pasteur & Galt Apothecary Shop carried a wide variety of medication and popular remedies of the day. Everything from herbs and elixirs to ointments and tinctures was prescribed by Dr. Galt, whose diplomas still hang in his shop.

Apothecary office. Surgical instruments used in amputations and operations are displayed.

Historic Area Stores

Nine Historic Area stores re-create the world of the colonial shopper. There's also a Colonial Nursery, where the kinds of plants found in colonial Williamsburg are sold and eighteenth-century gardening techniques are demonstrated.

Tarpley's Store delights visitors with a wide variety of colonial-style goods and souvenirs.

Outside, Tarpley's Store displays baskets and a window full of hats and caps.

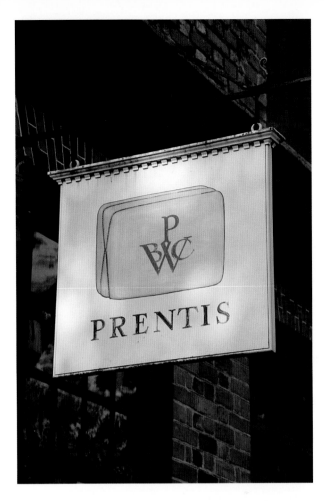

The Prentis Store is Williamsburg's best surviving example of a colonial store. Goods shipped to England by Prentis & Company would have borne the Prentis mark, shown here on the shop sign. Tea consigned to Prentis was thrown into the York River during the "Yorktown Tea Party" of November 1774.

The McKenzie Apothecary, located very near the Governor's Palace, on Palace Street.

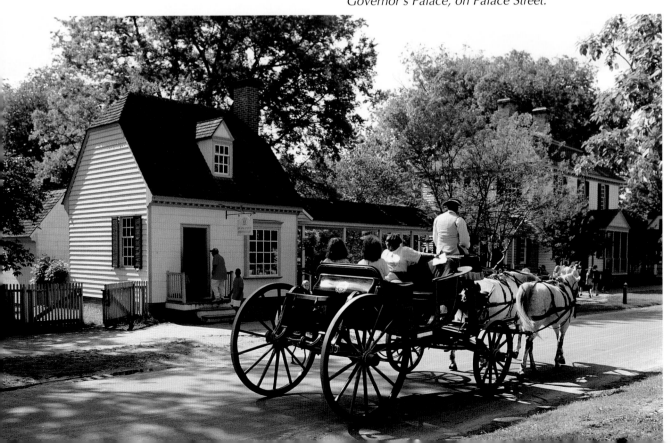

Inside the Greenhow Store, jars full of eighteenth-century-style candy and a display of cinnamon sticks greet visitors.

Hats hang outside the Mary Dickinson Store . . .

. . . where a woman in costume and the same style hat sweeps the sidewalk.

The time-honored customs, of hanging goods outside a store to attract attention . . .

. . . or posting a notice in the window to advertise newly arrived wares from England, are still evident in Colonial Williamsburg.

Just IMPORTED from London, And to be SOLD at a reasonable Advance for ready MONEY only.

COMPLETE Sets of BOTTLES and STAFFORDSHIRE WARE, fit for the FACULTY. Likewise PICKLING JARS of all Sorts for Family Use.

Merchants Square

Merchants Square is a large area located on the west end of town that is devoted to modern shopping and eating in quality restaurants. Here the emphasis is on superior goods sold in an old-world atmosphere.

Merchants Square is a commercial area that includes restaurants, stores, and the Williamsburg Theatre, a fine arts cinema showing foreign films and independent productions.

Storefronts are in keeping with the colonial tradition.

Restaurants serve a variety of good food both indoors and outdoors.

Carter's Grove Plantation
on the James River

The Carter's Grove mansion stands overlooking the James River, eight miles southeast of Colonial Williamsburg. A symbol of great colonial wealth, this Georgian-style house is a delightful combination of beautiful brickwork and masterful woodwork. Construction was originally started in 1750 by Carter Burwell, on property inherited from his grandfather, Robert "King" Carter, who had been the most powerful and wealthy tobacco planter in Virginia colony. King Carter's vast agricultural holdings had included some three hundred thousand acres. He originally bought the land at Carter's Grove for his daughter Elizabeth.

Basing his ideas on designs in architectural books received from London, Burwell organized the building of his own house and employed the skills of local brickmason David Minitree to construct the walls. Later Minitree also put glass into the mansion's 540 windowpanes. John Wheatly, another local craftsman, directed slaves and carpenters in the construction of timber framework for the floors and roof. In addition, a joiner, Richard Baylis, was brought from England with his family to work on the detailed interior woodwork with the help of local craftsmen. Two outbuildings, one on either end of the main house, served as a laundry and a kitchen, and were built during the 1740s. Hyphens that now connect these to the house were added much later, in the 1930s.

The house was completed in 1755, but unfortunately Burwell died soon afterwards. His estate then passed to his six-year-old son Nathaniel. By 1771, Nathaniel Burwell had come of age and assumed responsibility for both the house and the family's considerable plantation holdings. He married Susannah Grymes and together they raised eight children. Six were still alive when Susannah died in 1788. Nathaniel subsequently married a widow, Lucy Page Baylor, who already had six children of her own. Their marriage produced eight more children. The house passed down through this large family to Carter Burwell III and then eventually to his son Philip Lewis Carter Burwell, who sold the property. After five generations, Carter's Grove passed out of the Burwell family.

Thereafter the plantation was occupied and farmed by various owners, until 1928 when Mr. and Mrs. Archibald M. McCrea bought it. With the help of their architect, Duncan Lee, they set about extensively expanding and renovating their new purchase. The hyphens were added, joining the structures into one building, which now measures just over two hundred feet long. The roof line was raised to provide additional space in the garret and dormer windows were inserted to light these new rooms. While the McCreas installed all the modern conveniences of their day, they were working to restore Carter's Grove to what was viewed in the 1930s and 1940s as the colonial style. They purchased art and furnishings, and had the grounds landscaped, in what has come to be known as Colonial Revival style.

Mrs. McCrea died in 1960, and her will expressed a wish that Carter's Grove be maintained for the benefit of future generations. It was purchased by the Sealantic Fund, a Rockefeller-supported organization, for the Colonial Williamsburg Foundation, which now preserves this historic house and grounds for public exhibition.

Today visitors see this mansion depicted inside as it appeared while the McCreas lived there. The rooms are furnished with a fine collection of furniture, art, and rugs dating from the seventeenth to the twentieth century. Many of these pieces were bought by the McCreas and some came from places like Westover Plantation, which is nearby on the James River.

Impressive front elevation of the Carter's Grove mansion, facing south onto the James River.

The entrance hall with grand staircase, where, myth relates, a notorious British cavalry officer who wished to awaken his sleeping men billeted above, rode his horse up the staircase slashing at the banister rail with his saber. Now there was an actual person called Colonel Tarleton, and he happened to be bivouacked in the area during the war, and his first name was Banastre, but there the story ends. There is no proof that this event actually occurred, but there are some very convincing scars that appear to be deep cuts at intervals up the length of the banister rail. Regardless of this story's worth, there is no doubting the splendid craftsmanship that went into making this impressive staircase, which must have been among the grandest in the land.

This comfortable and beautifully furnished room is commonly called the "Refusal Room," because unsubstantiated legend has it that this is where both George Washington and Thomas Jefferson, on different occasions and with different women, were refused their proposals of marriage.

Occupying the west hyphen, this bright sitting room's furniture is relatively modern.

Located in the west wing, the smoking room was a favorite with the McCrea family and demonstrates their love for recreation. With blackout curtains drawn, Mrs. McCrea spent many evenings playing solitaire in this room during World War II.

The dining room.

TOP LEFT: *Servant's hall, which is attached to the east hyphen and contains civil defense paraphernalia for an interpretation of life at the mansion during World War II.*

TOP RIGHT: *Butler's pantry, with World War II ration books.*

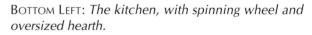

BOTTOM LEFT: *The kitchen, with spinning wheel and oversized hearth.*

BOTTOM RIGHT: *A servant's quarters, with rudimentary furnishings.*

A 1930s Hotpoint electric stove must have been state of the art at the time.

This paneled library is richly furnished.

Drawing room, furnished in opulent Colonial Revival style. The beautiful paneling is original but would have been painted during the eighteenth century.

The morning porch with its river view is located in the east hyphen and was an ideal place to take breakfast.

Upstairs in the east hyphen is a cleverly laid out guest dressing room and bathroom, under a sloping roof amidst dormer windows.

Water closets are unobtrusively placed behind pan-eled doors.

One of two quaint mirrored dressing tables built into recesses.

Accessories and military uniforms depict the 1940s in this inviting guest room, with its pink silk bed curtains.

This large room upstairs over the front hall was Mr. McCrea's office.

Mr. and Mrs. McCrea's bedrooms are located upstairs, in the west wing, which afforded them complete privacy. This is Mrs. McCrea's bedroom.

Mr. McCrea's bedroom.

Slave Quarter
at Carter's Grove

Reconstructed on a site unearthed during archaeological digs, the dwellings, garden plots, and animal pens now on show reveal much about life as a slave on an eighteenth-century plantation. Original storage pits discovered in the ground indicated where structures were built. These would have been the homes and barns of agricultural and skilled African-American workers who tended the land at Carter's Grove.

An interpreter is on hand to guide visitors through the quarter.

Inside a primitive dwelling showing a slave's possessions.

A barn with tobacco drying.

Layout of the slave quarter with a patch of garden.

Wolstenholme Towne
at Carter's Grove

With partial support from the National Geographic Society, the Colonial Williamsburg Foundation excavated a site of an English settlement located here on Carter's Grove, which was originally known as Martin's Hundred. Established in 1619, the settlement was called Wolstenholme Towne but it was abandoned three years later after an Indian attack in which many of the inhabitants were either killed or carried off.

Lying hidden for more than three centuries, the unearthed foundations of the buildings have now been redefined and a wooden fort partially reconstructed. Audio presentations allow visitors to relive the town's history.

This site is located in a flat meadow on the banks of the James River and is a pleasant walk from the Carter's Grove mansion.

Redefined outlines of the Wolstenholme Towne settlement buildings.

The partially reconstructed wooden fort.

Winthrop Rockefeller Archaeology Museum
at Carter's Grove

At the entrance to the Winthrop Rockefeller Archaeology Museum a plaque reads: Focused on the archaeology and history of the early colonial settlement of Martin's Hundred, the museum helps us begin the journey into the 17th century that ends on the site of Wolstenholme Towne, where many of the exhibited artifacts were found.

Located underground in a hillside is this excellent archaeological museum portraying seventeenth-century Tidewater life with valuable excavated artifacts. It is a beautiful, rich account of the archaeological finds unearthed at Wolstenholme Towne.

Wall displays with maps, drawings, documents, and detailed information are accompanied by audio interpretations. Exhibits include weapons, farming tools, crops and food, household implements, and items of apparel, as well as layouts of buildings. All clearly illustrate the experiences of the early settlers of Martin's Hundred.

Demonstrating the necessity for strong fortifications when settling in an area threatened by Indians and the Spanish, the building of Wolstenholme Town and its fort is also shown in great detail.

Path leading to the underground exhibit halls.

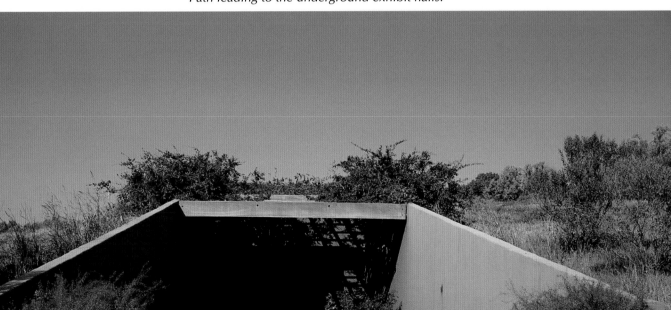

A display and an ancient cannon found at the site.

Restored helmets retrieved from archaeological excavations at Wolstenholme Towne site. There is an interesting movie explaining the recovery of these artifacts showing in a room adjacent to the exhibit.

Visitors with cars may return to Colonial Williamsburg via the Country Road, a one-way picturesque tidewater drive, seven miles long. It passes through woodlands and over marshes and tidal creeks.

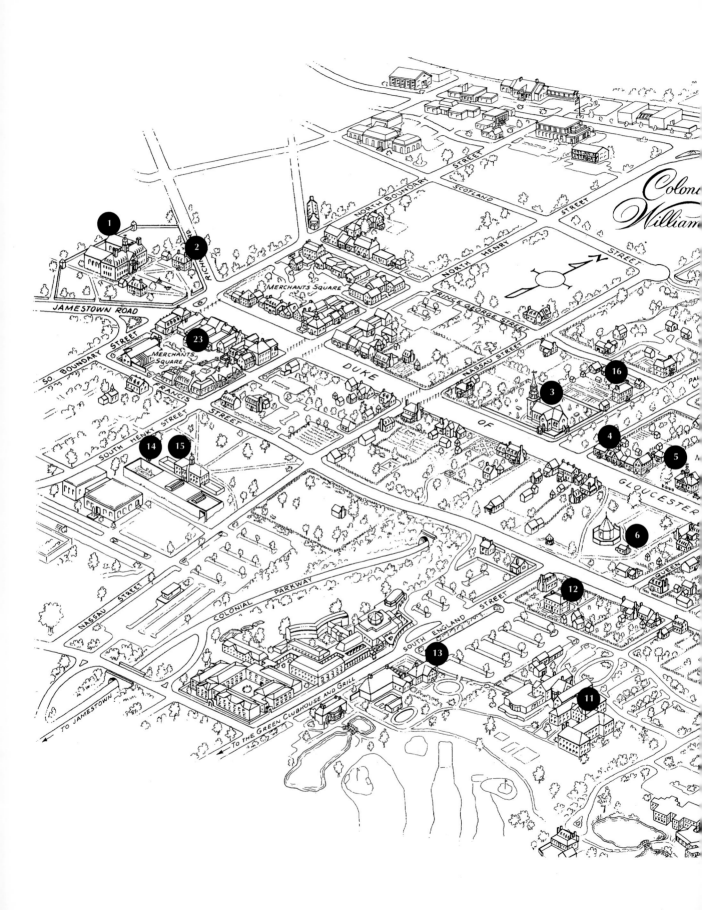

MAP KEY

1. Wren Building
2. President's House
3. Bruton Parish Church
4. James Geddy House
5. Courthouse
6. Magazine and Guardhouse
7. Wetherburn's Tavern
8. Raleigh Tavern
9. Capitol
10. Bassett Hall
11. Williamsburg Inn
12. Lightfoot House
13. Abby Aldrich Rockefeller Folk Art Center
14. DeWitt Wallace Gallery
15. Public Hospital
16. George Wythe House
17. Governor's Palace
18. Brush-Everard House
19. Robertson's Windmill
20. Peyton Randolph House
21. Public Gaol
22. Benjamin Powell House
23. Merchants Square
24. Carter's Grove

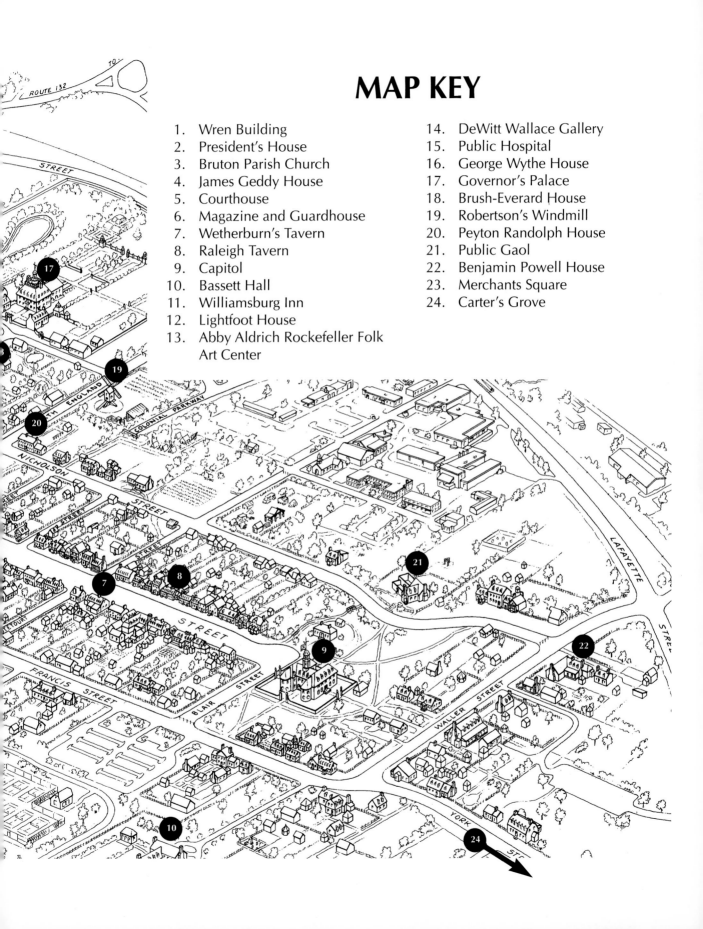

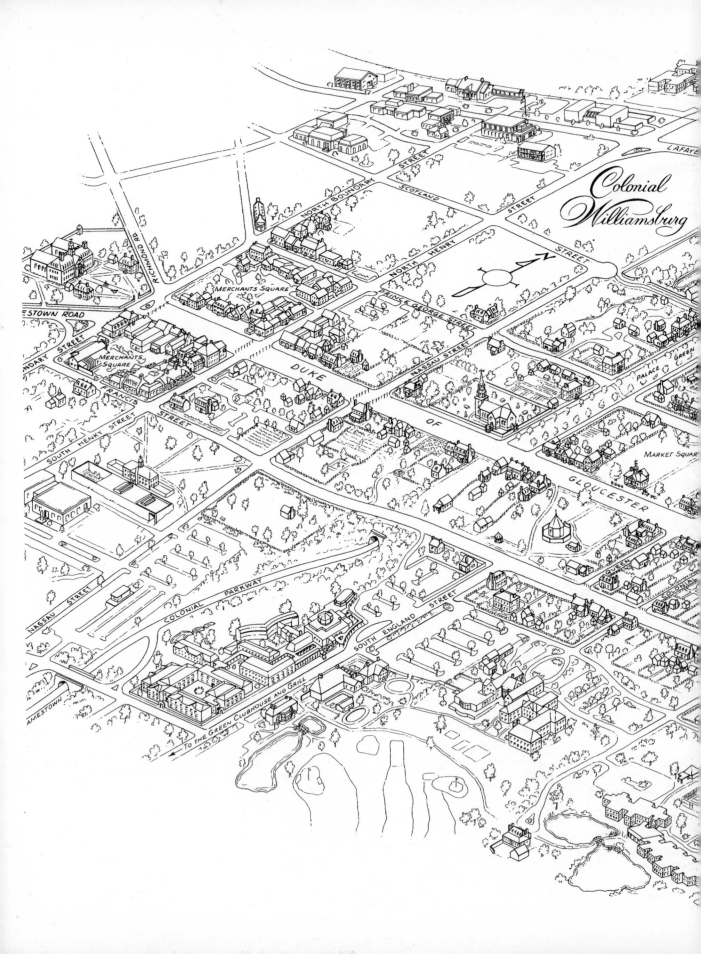

Colonial Williamsburg